IN
   ALL SPACES
         LIMINAL

Copyright © 2025
Cover art by Prisha Kudikala

All rights reserved. No part of this publication may be reproduced, distributed, or transmitted in any form or by any means, including photocopying, recording, or other electronic or mechanical methods, without the prior written permission of the author, except in the case of brief quotations embodied in critical reviews and certain other noncommercial uses permitted by copyright law.

The Seattle Youth Poet Laureate is a special program of Seattle Arts & Lectures in partnership with Urban Word.

ISBN 978-1-949166-11-8

Published by Poetry NW Editions
2000 Tower Street
Everett, WA 98201

Distributed by Ingram

PRINTED IN THE UNITED STATES OF AMERICA

Seattle Youth Poet Laureate Series No. 10

IN
ALL SPACES
LIMINAL

JANAE LU

Liminal is derived from the Latin "limen," meaning threshold. It is a place of transition, a time of waiting, and not knowing the future. It is the space between where you have been and where you will go, when what comes next is still uncertain. Liminality is not arrival or conclusion but the state of becoming. This collection exists in that space: between past and future, presence and absence, holding on and letting go.

Contents

Tell Me, What Is It You Plan to Do with
   Your One Wild and Precious Life? _____ 1

Ode to Seattle _____ 2

School Has Just Started, and I Am Already Tired _____ 3

Molecular Theory _____ 4

August _____ 5

Astronomers Say That from Our Point of View, We'll Always Look
   Like We're in the Center of the Universe _____ 7

They Tell You Your New Life Will Cost You Your Old One _____ 8

Ballad of a High Schooler Who Dreams of Restarting Their Life _____ 9

It's the Time of the Year When All Therapists Have Waitlists _____ 10

Savior Complex _____ 11

Lessons in Anatomy _____ 12

An Ode to the Sadness I Hold Inside This Body _____ 14

Escape Velocity _____ 16

When Rest Turned into Something I Had to Afford _____ 17

Who's to Blame? _____ 19

There It Is Again, That Funny Feeling _____ 20

February Tasted Like Black Coffee and Second Guesses _____ 21

The Space I Take Up (and How I Wish It Was Smaller) _____ 22

STATUS UPDATE: Janae Lu is feeling fine _____ 23

Handmade Humanity _____ 24

Kaleidoscope _____ 26

I Have a Fantasy Where Everyone I Love Sits at the Same Dining Room Table	27
The Doctor Put Her Hand Over My Liver and Told Me My Resentment Is Getting Smaller	28
Five-Year Plan	29
Acknowledgments	31
About the Author	33

Tell Me, What Is It You Plan to Do with Your One Wild and Precious Life?

After Mary Oliver

It is the hottest day of the year. The heat reaches its lazy body over the surface of all things. It's stagnant but somehow stays moving. Small insects interrupt the stillness, their wings sending ripples, making leaves shudder.

July is nearing expiration, and I am torn between feeling everything and not caring at all. There is so much time; there is nothing left. It matters, and yet, still, it doesn't.

I'm staring at a blue swatch of sky and imagining every option at once. I could stay here, in the grass, for a decade, spine parallel to the earth. I could be far away, if I wanted. I could die in the next minute. I could live forever, somewhere else. I could stand up, stretch, take the trash out, cut bangs, rearrange my bedroom, read a book. Raise a child: feed it, nurture it, watch it grow. Sit at a desk, stare at a screen. Buy a sailboat. Go to school. Teach myself how to crochet. Pluck a few words out of the brambles in my brain and arrange them into strings of sentences. Loudly declare *this is who I am!* and try to convince myself it's honest.

Something in me is telling myself to be gentle, that we don't need know, we don't need to have a plan. But there is something else, something more urgent. It pounds, like a pulse, like a timer: *hurry, please, this is all you have.*

Ode to Seattle

The sun breaks Seattle
into shattered shadows,
the bulging city streets twisting
a rattlesnake's fight uphill. We dig
our heels into callous concrete
ready to fall on our hands.

We know the smells well:
the ports' bright brine, the wafts of sewage,
and the sweet musk of borrowed
books: yellowed from
years of sea damp, cool dark, in our hands.
They sigh, the wonderful relief of
a long-held breath.

This city,
this crooked, dirty place,
was once the center of a smaller world.
I know well, this city,
my foggy first love:
in romantic remembrance,
in regretful afterthought,
in limb ripping homesickness.

Heartbreak too, I know well —
it happens just once,
then no other city
will ever hurt as much.

School Has Just Started, and I Am Already Tired

The cycle widens its hungry, drooling mouth
and swallows what is left of my time.
I feel the exhaustion in my bone marrow,
my jaw, the faltering pulse in my wrist.
I yearn to pull sleep around myself
like soil cradling a grave.
Tuck me in, leave me there
until I'm different, better.

I have memorized the way
the sunrise comes in sideways
through my bedroom windows —
each photon like a proof,
you're awake, you're awake, you're awake.
Films play on the insides of my eyelids:
hands cupped around my cheeks,
chests growing with full breaths,
lips parted, bodies calm.
It all feels like it lives on the other side
of the haze, past the boundary
between here, and the things I deserve.

I've stared at this fatigue for so long
that its edges have started to blur.
Framed, in full focus,
I am afraid it is the only thing that exists.

Molecular Theory

I read something once that claimed
it is theoretically possible for one solid mass
to pass entirely through another —
it's something about the placement of atoms
and the spaces they leave in their wake.
Supposedly, when you least expect it,
your hand is capable of passing right through
your bedroom wall, or your bathroom mirror,
or your own body.

How often do we think something is stable?
How often do we turn out to be wrong?
How many times have I watched my own reaching fingers
pass straight through those who I thought were steadfast?
How common is that disconnect *really*?

I've adopted this habit where I repeatedly tap
on the surface of the things that are near me,
watching my own atoms collide with all the others.
It's happened before, I promise.
I've had unwavering things —
the tangible, the touchable, the permanent —
and I've watched their dispersion, their detachment,
and all the emptiness that emerges
when you least expect it.

August

After Taylor Swift

August slipped away
into a moment in time.
It was carried downstream
with the last of the glacier water,
in some direction opposite of mine.

I watch from the riverbank as the threshold
between day and night readjusts itself.
The sun sets at seven and the cold cloak
of autumn has begun to wrap itself around
my corner of the world.
Frost creeps in fractals up car windows
and formerly lush green hillsides
drench themselves in amber.

The season changes with no regard
to those experiencing it.
Life does not stop for us;
it doesn't have to.
There is envy

in my admiration of nature
and her ability to be so fluid.
She understands nothing of confinement
and does not weep over her losses,
knowing they'll come back if they're meant to.

Someday, I will learn to let go,
and live the way she does:
ever-evolving, ever-growing,
flowing with the tide,
falling with the rain,
changing with the leaves.

Astronomers Say That from Our Point of View, We'll Always Look Like We're in the Center of the Universe

Because the far-away light is reaching us equivalently in all directions. Time has allowed us a radius that is only so wide — teleport a few trillion miles away, and you'll still be in the same-sized sphere.

What I mean is you're trapped in the focal point: the only life you'll ever see is the one you're forced to be in the middle of. We are eight billion legitimate centers, with histories like revolving doors, bicycle spokes, celestial bodies. Every one of us is the end of the tether, the common denominator.

What I mean is I've never had another option: I am the only choice I have, and here I am, immobile and motion sick, watching revolutions from the spotlight, everything that ever happens blurring into streaks.

What I mean is sometimes I don't want to be here: with the recognizable patterns and the predictable paths of travel, remembering each shape, each unfathomably far object that returns to me every now and then.

What I mean is we aren't allowed to detach: even if we hate it, we are bound entirely to ourselves.

They Tell You Your New Life Will Cost You Your Old One

But they never tell you your old one
will still have half a heartbeat.
The pulse is slow, but it is there.
Your old life will scratch at your door
like an abandoned animal, whimpering —
a constant reminder that you left someone behind.
It will find ways to creep into your peripheral
like poison ivy —
silent, evident, and untouchable.

And they don't tell you there are still ways to return to it.
You'll find her old bottle of perfume at the back of your closet
and the scent will shoot you back to two years ago.
You'll meet strangers with her name
and try not to feel unsettled as you shake their hands.

The home you ran from is still standing.
The mother you loved is still alive.

And they always forget to mention the nights
you'll spend cross-legged on your bedroom floor,
surrounded by all the family photos you cut yourself out of.
Staring at the you-shaped outline in the foreground,
you'll wonder what it truly means to be better off.

Ballad of a High Schooler
Who Dreams of Restarting Their Life
After Sylvia Plath

You know what it's like to walk into a room,
and first think of the easiest way to leave it.
You daydream of fleeing to a cabin in the forest,
or a faraway island, or some other planet
where you can be satisfied.
It's not here, though, it's not this,
it's somewhere else, somewhere else, somewhere else.

You've been running since you learned
how much farther it could take you,
and yes, you're fast,
and sure, you're far,
but now the ground feels wrong
when you stand still upon it.

So you sift frantic and focused
through every potential, every timeline,
like your ideal lies in a pile of old family photographs,
or amidst a display of name-shaped keychains —
if you saw it, if you could only find it,
you would know: this one is yours.

Somewhere else there exists the life that means the most;
it hangs heavy like the fig from the end of a tree branch,
waiting to reveal itself.
You'll pluck it from the masses,
and it will fit, round and right in your palm.

It's the Time of the Year When All Therapists Have Waitlists

Sometimes we are lucky enough to see the sun.
She comes out for a few hours
and then leaves by four p.m. without saying goodbye.
When I ask her to stay,
she does not respond.
I sit like a dog at the living room window
waiting for her to return.

I wish I could tell you I've been gone
because I've been tending to wounds
instead of avoiding them.
I'd love to show you all the hours I've slept
and the breakfasts I've eaten.
You'd see me as something purified,
like I came out of the dark as a new body.

I've emerged, I am different,
everything is better now.

I fantasize about framing the four p.m. light
from the living room window.
I'd trap it between panes of glass
and hang it on the wall for the next few months.

The leaves would fall
and the world would lose its color
but at least, through every tired hour,
we'd still have this.

Savior Complex

I keep having this nightmare
where every person I have ever loved
is standing on a fishing dock.
Their hands are tied behind their backs
as they make painful small talk with one another
trying to understand why they're there.
I'm watching from a boat with two seats:
one for me, one left empty someone else.

Suddenly they're all yelling,
each desperate voice harmonizing into collective urgency.
Water floods the dock, filling their shoes
and welling up around their calves.
Come quick! they say as the lake swallows their waists,
their chests, their shoulders.
Help me, let me be the one you save.
I loved you the most.

But I don't save anyone.
I sit in my boat, and I don't move
until they're all underwater.
Potential sinks from view.

I stare at the ripples until I wake up.
(You can analyze this all you want).
(I already know what it means).

Lessons in Anatomy

I.
The human brain is seventy-nine cubic inches in volume.
Everything you have ever known
fits into seventy-nine cubic inches of headspace.

II.
The first lobotomy was performed in 1946.
Since then, there have been over 50,000 lobotomies in the
U.S.
and I have had dozens of them.
In moments when I feel particularly unwell,
I disconnect my frontal lobe and try to rearrange the clutter.
I've been told it's supposed to help stabilize a personality.
I can tell you I've been trying to map these
seventy-nine cubic inches
for my entire life, and I still don't understand where I am.

III.
There's something so incredibly lonely
about the fact that our consciousnesses cannot be shared.
So badly have I wanted to take a piece of myself
and let another person carry it for a while:
to make this load a little lighter,
not to tell you, but to show you instead.

IV.
There is a special type of solitude that is found
when you become trapped in your own skull.
Think: you are stranded on a desert island.
Think: you are lost in space.
Think: you are all you have.

An Ode to the Sadness I Hold Inside This Body

Thin and ever-present,
it lives as a vein inside some inconspicuous piece of earth.
Crack me open, hold me up to the light,
and find it hiding there.

On the harder days, I feel the topography of my face change.
Some of these lines weren't here before —
these trenches between my eyebrows
and these caverns beneath my cheekbones.
Two more weeks
and this landscape will erode into unrecognition.

Last summer I would have written
some light-hearted little line
about acceptance and how it's important
in situations like these:
>*There will always be a part of you*
>*that holds sadness, my dear.*
>*Don't fight it off.*
>*Let its weight make you stronger.*

But I am sick of acceptance.
I don't want to carry it anymore.
I want to mine the vein,
extract the toxins,
and be clean again.

I am waiting for the moment when I can detach it,
grip the root and pull,
untangle this old growth from the rest of my organs,
and live with a little more room inside my chest.
I am waiting,
        I am waiting,
                I am waiting.

Escape Velocity

I've been spending a lot of time thinking
about the first person who went out into earth's orbit.
More recently it feels like my good days
are strapped atom bombs —
a countdown to an explosion
that I'll spend the next week recovering from.
They blast all the pigment out of my planet and leave me
with nothing but dust to rebuild with.

You tell me this is just how life is:
phases of technicolor between monochrome droughts,
but when everything dulls like this,
I imagine ripping the world into black and white fragments
and throwing them all back at you.
Take your fleeting moments,
I want something that won't leave.

I've been spending a lot of time thinking
about the first person who went out into earth's orbit,
and how he was so much more courageous than me.
Not because he cast himself in a jostling, burning, hunk of metal,
or because he survived the suffocating lack of oxygen,
or even because he risked losing everything he had ever loved
for a few lines in history,
but because when he peaked —
zero gravity, 100,000 feet up —
he looked down at the space below
and had the strength to come back down.

When Rest Turned into Something I Had to Afford

The last time I was sick like this,
I used thumbtacks to pin my top sheet over my bedroom
     window.
My face was burning holes through my pillowcases
and my lungs had melted into the rest of my organs.

My mother visited for the first time in three years.
She brought a doctor with her.
together, they held their icy hands against my cheeks
and told me I was dying.
I believed them.
When I woke up, they were gone.
I was alone in an empty home.
They were only ghosts.

Flash forward to this moment:
I'm writing this in my head,
with my bare shoulders pressed into the floor of my bathtub.
This time, there are no dreams to keep me company.

I used to joke about wishing I'd get sick,
just so I could take a break.
How nice it would be to close my eyes for a full day.
How nice it would be to heal.

Instead, I'm here, tossing back cough syrup
and stringing lines of poetry together
under this stream of burning water.

I'll be here until I sweat the fever out
or until the ghosts come back.
Whichever comes first.

Who's to Blame?

I. I loved you,
The first time I drowned,
I was four years old.
The ocean invited me in, tempting
me with its ribbons of waves.
It wrapped itself around my calves
and licked the tips of my fingers.

II. but I wasn't afraid to lose you like the others.
The current tied itself around my limbs
as I was pulled underwater,
suddenly enveloped in fluid ice
and thrown against the shore.
The sand that once felt soft
now left bruises.

III. Though I think that has less to do with you,
The air in my lungs was stolen,
stripped, replaced
with something more dense.
A mouth surrounded by inaccessible oxygen.
A body close to the surface,
but too weak to reach it.

IV. and more to do with me.
My chest still aches when I think about it.
That could be the heartbreak,
but I'll blame the saltwater.

There It Is Again, That Funny Feeling

After Bo Burnham

Googled derealization, hated what I found.
A couple hundred forests fell, but did they make a sound?
Survival of the fittest, losing interest, *come home soon*,
shooting for the stars and somehow landing on the moon.

Watch yourself get older, warmer, colder, a whole new face,
standing with your feet planted in someone else's place.
Time taking bites of calendars, head hung above the sink.
Come and get your fortune read, it's darker than you'd think.
All flags flown at half mast, driving too fast, here we go:
we're all in this together and we're all in this alone.

Harsh lights at the hospital, car heater on full blast,
sprinkles of chipped nail polish, pieces of your past.
Five missed calls from family, *doing badly, can this wait?*
A thousand tiny question marks all piled upon your plate.
Staring contests with your ceiling, words you can't pronounce,
waking up from nightmares to a silent, empty house.
Working for tomorrow, but today won't come to a close.
Count down from ten and back again:
oxygen overdose.

February Tasted Like Black Coffee and Second Guesses

It budded and brewed
and brought an ending
so catastrophic that it turned the middle obsolete
(I've learned it's so hard to remember
the lay of our land when I visit
after its downfall).

Recently I have been accompanied
by this incomprehensible sadness.
This is not to say it is massive or disabling,
rather it purely refuses to be understood —
boiling it down leaves me with nothing
but murky water and unanswered texts.

I'm tired of living with my hands
hovering above the steering wheel.
I want to hold things in confidence,
to grasp tightly to something and know
truly, honestly, and completely
that it belongs to me.

With February comes the decline of the calendar
and this familiar itch of uncertainty.
Winter releases deep exhale
and I sigh alongside her.
Another month has bloomed and withered,
and we still don't know
which way we're headed.

The Space I Take Up
(and How I Wish It Was Smaller)

And how I wish it didn't matter so much to me.
Some days, I catch myself eating
beauty standards for breakfast.
Later, I fall asleep with a mouth full
of excuses and a stomach stuffed
with yearning.

I watch my reflection as she thinks about this.
She grips her own sides
and wishes they would retreat inwards,
wills them to fade until they disappear,
until there is nothing left,
until the space she takes up
is nearly unnoticeable.

I ask her how she can expect these things.
How she can even attempt to contain everything she is
in the notch of a belt.
I tell her that her worth
is not measured by her waistline,
that you cannot weigh potential on a scale,
and that her words cannot be read
if there is not a body here to write them.
I tell her this and can only hope
that she is listening.

STATUS UPDATE:
Janae Lu is feeling fine

Janae Lu is up past her bedtime. Janae Lu is having a staring contest with her bedroom wall. Janae Lu is thinking about how when you repeat the same phrases over and over it starts to sound foreign. Janae Lu is looking for a distraction. Is working too hard. Is not working hard enough. Janae Lu would like to invite you to her balancing act. To watch her teeter on tightropes. To watch her juggle all her lives. Janae Lu is looking for recommendations on how to stay upright. On the Great American Novel. On how to care less about what people think. Janae Lu is sinking her teeth into her tongue. Is practicing restraint. Is deleting lines.

Janae Lu has written her name so many times it has started to lose meaning. Is trying to make sense of it. Does not want you to worry.

Will be alright.

Handmade Humanity

Whoever created me gave me this unshakable unsatisfaction,
a need to prove that I have improved since you saw me yesterday,
and this existence on the fine line between caring too much
and not caring at all
because none of this really matters, does it?

They called me finished after they dragged the wet bristles
of a paintbrush across the beds of my eyes,
staining me purple with fatigue
and chuckling to themselves
as they watch my never-ending attempts to conceal it.

They took all the unwanted rubble
from my past lives and melded it
into bones, like some karmic result
that presents itself with soft skin and jutted angles.

They declared that everything that ever was,
will be related to everything that has ever been,
and that everything my eyes touch
will be a reminder of something else.

*She will never stop
thinking or yearning or running.
Fear will both deflate and inspire her,
and she will spend her life wondering
about fields of greener grasses and
the people that tend to them.*

And when all was said and done,
when everything had been sanded, primed, and painted,
they cast my body into the center of a jagged mountain range
and dared me to find my own way out.

No direction, no instruction, just out.

Kaleidoscope

It is spring.
The poets' hearts are thawing
as if they didn't spend the last four months
convinced they were cracked beyond recognition.

Every year is like this:
winter freezes us senseless,
shows us how numb we can be,
and then disappears overnight.

It leaves us dumbfounded,
staring at the pollen sprinkled delicately
on our windshields like it's something supernatural.
We've spent centuries here
but are somehow still surprised
when the birds come back.

My life, all at once, is massive and microscopic.
I am a billion parts of an infinite thing.
The floor of my home is scattered
with squares of warm sunlight.
The neighbor's daffodils nod their heads at one another.

I welcome the moments,
keeping them company
until they stand to leave,
and after they go,
I leave the door open
to let new air in.

I Have a Fantasy Where Everyone I Love Sits at the Same Dining Room Table

The air smells like sage, and the candlelight is dimming because the wicks were lit so long ago. There is laughter that comes from the bottom of the stomach; there are absentminded smiles. My shoulders do not naturally curl inward like a late November leaf. No one is missing; every seat is filled. Someone passes a plate to the person next to them. When a glass slips from a hand and shatters on the hardwood, it is met with one single apology and half a dozen voices saying *hey, don't worry about it, everything is just fine.*

We never learned what it means to fight or how it feels to hang up without saying goodbye. Instead, someone asks me if I've tried any new recipes lately. They ask me to recommend a book for them. They ask if I've had enough to eat.

For a brief moment, I catch the melted shapes of all our reflections in the window. I stare until we are no longer separate entities, until we are one watercolor blur, until there is nothing I would change.

The Doctor Put Her Hand Over My Liver and Told Me My Resentment Is Getting Smaller

After Phoebe Bridgers

It's been three years or maybe six days,
or maybe my entire eternity,
I do not remember.
The memory is eroding with everything else —
shrinking, collapsing, like stars dying, drying up.
After the resentment leaves, I am mostly empty space.

In my peripheral, your wake looks gentle.
You look best as blurred lines,
approachable only as shapeless cool tones

with no harsh edges or pollution to forgive.
They say acceptance is the stitch
that pulls the wound closed.
I tell them I am decorated in embroidery.

The doctor ran her fingers
along my collection of tightened thread
and told me my history is healing.

It's been three years or maybe six days,
or maybe my entire eternity,
I am forgetting, little by little
you are fading out,
like stars dying,
like a knot pulled finally tight.

Five-Year Plan

Care a little less. Maybe significantly less. Underline more books. Dog-ear more pages. Spend more time in the sun, get to know her. Quit smoking (if I start). Start writing (if I quit). Vacuum the rug, lay on it for a minute or two. Confront my demons, invite them out to dinner. Collect poems for a daughter I don't have. Apologize appropriately. Plant more seeds in the ground. Make bad art. Overpay for lemonade at a stand run by the neighborhood kids. Walk the dog. Identify the highest point in the world, climb it, and throw my phone off the top. Go back to sending letters, long ones, with hearts drawn in the margins and crimson wax seals. Take the long way home. Forgive in a way that makes forgetting irrelevant. Search for peace, find it in the backyard. Ask *what do you think?* Say *we should do this more often.* Wear sunscreen. Leave my fingerprints on everything, mark the world with evidence that proves I was here, and here, and here. Tell people that I love them. Breathe in, breathe out. Carry on.

Carry on.

Carry on.

Acknowledgments

Seattle Arts & Lectures: Thank you for dreaming this program into existence, for believing in the necessity of young voices, and offering a home for words before they even know what they wish to become.

Poetry NW Editions: Thank you for giving these words a life beyond the fragile edges of my mind. For your care, your generosity, and for ensuring my poetry can live on a page.

Jourdan Imani Keith and Nanya Jhingran: Thank you for your wisdom, insight, and grace for me in this journey. Your mentorship has shaped both this collection and the poet I am still becoming.

Indira Dahlstrom: Thank you for your generosity, kindness, and unwavering support. Your encouragement and the opportunities you have provided have meant the world to me.

Adhi Kona: Thank you for setting this story into motion. I can trace it back to a single moment — freshman year, Christensen's room, your voice in rehearsal — and from there, something in me shifted and I have never stopped writing since. You have been with me through every version of myself, through every draft, every reading, every step of this winding path. No words could ever be enough to express the depth of my gratitude, but if poetry has taught me anything, it is that I will spend a lifetime trying.

Ms. Fort: Thank you for being the first adult in my life to truly believe in me. Your love for literature shaped not only the writer I have become but also the way I see the world. You introduced me to the power of words, encouraged me to take myself seriously as a poet, and made space for my voice when I was still learning how to use it. From helping me refine my work to rehearsing readings with me, from offering thoughtful edits on this collection to sharing books that changed the way I write, your guidance has been invaluable. I will always treasure our conversations, your wisdom, and the unwavering support you have given me.

Mr. Mickelson: Thank you for your kindness, your encouragement, and the generosity with which you offer your time and wisdom. You have helped me craft this collection with both precision and care. Whether in poetry or prose, you have taught me to pay attention — to structure, to meaning, to the weight of every sentence. Your confidence in me has strengthened my own, and for that, I am endlessly grateful.

Prisha Kudikala: Thank you for being my constant and standing beside me through every season of my life. You have let me drag you to poetry readings, listened patiently to my endless musings, and held space for me even when my words made little sense. Your support has never been conditional, and your friendship has been one of the greatest gifts. And beyond all of that, you gave this book its face — you turned words into something tangible, something that can be held. Just as you have always been there, steady and certain, your work now stands beside mine, and I will cherish that always.

About the Author

Janae Lu is a writer whose work explores the nuances of transition, identity, and self-discovery through free-verse poetry and creative prose. She is the 2024-25 Seattle Youth Poet Laureate, a junior at Tesla STEM High School, the chair of the Redmond Teen Advisory Board, and a second-year member of the Seattle Youth Poetry Fellowship. When not writing she can be found doing endless amounts of homework, overanalyzing Taylor Swift lyrics, and adding to her forever growing book collection.

This book is set in Century Old Style STD

Book design by Cara Sutherland with assistance from
Indira Dahlstrom and Abi Pollokoff

Produced and published by Poetry NW Editions,
an educational press in the Written Arts Program
at Everett Community College

www.ingramcontent.com/pod-product-compliance
Lightning Source LLC
Chambersburg PA
CBHW052127070526
44586CB00016B/2123